This Little Book Belongs to:

_____

_____

Dedicated to:

Every single reader of this little book who ever has or ever will face a struggle big or small. You are ALL warriors and my HERO for being you!

-XO Jessycka Drew

Butterflies & String, 2020
Series: Little Books for Little Warriors Volume 2
Written and illustrated by Jessycka Drew

Copyright © 2020 Jessycka Drew
All rights reserved.
MotherButterfly Books
www.motherbutterfly.com

This edition is published by arrangement with Jessycka Drew.
All Rights Reserved. No part of this publication may be reproduced or transmitted in any form or by any means, electronic or mechanical, including photocopying, recording, or any information storage and retrieval systems, without permission in writing from the publisher.

Requests for permission to make copies of any part of this work should be submitted online at www.motherbutterfly.com

ISBN 978-1-989579-12-1
ebook ISBN 78-1-989579-13-8

www.motherbutterfly.com

laugh.learn.love

Butterflies & String

From The Imaginative World of Jessycka Drew

Greetings Dear One, from Jessycka Drew.
I write little books with messages to YOU!

My little books

give you some help
with all sorts of things
that may come about.

For Little warriors who are so very tough
but need a little help getting through tough stuff.
Each book is for one very tough thing,
that a little warrior is battling.

Every book ends with hope

and special tools to help you cope.

Tips & Tricks

Tips & tricks are tools for you

like a sword, shield, and armour too.

You'll have what you need to fight

and face tough stuff with all your might.

This little book has a message to bring
to help you with an unpleasant thing.
It's called

"Anxiety"

a not so very fun feeling

that I have renamed...

These knotty butterflies
and their knotted string
give you a feeling
that's quite frightening!

They bring their string
and tie it all up.
They get in your belly
right in your gut!

The feeling can come without any warning.
It can happen at night, midday,
or the morning.

It happens sometimes for no reason at all,
or when you are scared
like when you might fall.

It's not your fault, Dear One.
Do you know?
Everyone gets anxious!
I know this is so.

I have a trick
that may give you some help
when those knotty butterflies
& string come about.

These butterflies follow an
unbreakable rule.
Remember this fact
it's your magical tool.

Unbreakable Rule

They can't stay forever,
they must go away.
If you catch them my dear,
this is what you should say.

"Knotty butterflies,
you don't have much time.
You can't stay forever, soon I'll be fine!
I'm stronger than you, so here is the thing...
You cannot hurt me with your silly string!"

Each and every time
you overcome your fears
you grow
Stronger
and
Stronger
and
Stronger
my Dear!

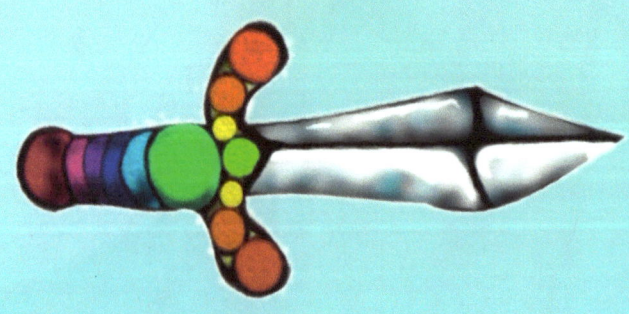

You can't be defeated
I know this is so!
Because you are a **warrior**,
Dear One, don't you know?

THE END...

...well almost the end.
There's TIPS & TRICKS, don't forget.
This little book isn't over yet.

Mirror mirror on the wall YOU are the mostest of them all!

When you are feeling sad, angry, or blue,
look into the mirror and say this to YOU!
Repeat this over and over to you...
Because it is so unbelievably true!
READY?!
Are you looking directly at you?!
Don't be shy...
Here we go!

Mirror Mirror on the Wall

You can't be defeated
I know this is so!

Because you are a
WARRIOR!

Don't you know?

You Are Beautiful!

The Name Game

When you think of "Anxiety" in your head, you may have feelings of yucky dread.

So picture something more FUN instead! Changing the name of an unpleasant thing can take away some of the sting.

Like changing "Anxiety" into:

Butterflies & String

The Name Game

Use this machine to play a game!

Your imagination can change any name.

Insert the name of anything at all that is yucky, not fun, or may make your skin crawl.

Send it through the imagination compactor.

Write or draw the brand new name any way you'd like, it's your game!

Imagination is the name of the game. That makes a name not at all the same!

Unbreakable Rule

Remember that trick that may give you some help
when those knotty butterflies come about?

You know the law,
it's your magical tool
to remind them of the UNBREAKABLE RULE.

They can't stay forever,
they must go away
you have the power,
tell them they can't stay!

If you catch them my Dear,
this is what you must say:

"Knotty butterflies,
you don't have much time.
You can't stay forever,
soon I'll be fine!
I'm stronger than you,
so here is the thing...
You cannot hurt me with your silly string!"

Knotty Butterflies
& their silly string
can't stay
forever they
must go away!

More Books in the Little Books for Little Warriors Series

About the Author

Born in Winslow, AZ and raised on the shores of Massachusetts, Jessycka Drew has developed a strong passion for art therapy. With a degree in social work, Jessycka has been passionately working in the field of human services.

Jessycka combines her love of helping others and her love of art by creating.

GO TO:

motherbutterfly.com/littlewarriors

for your FREE book!

Loved this Book?

Sharing is Caring!

Please share the love by leaving a review online.

THANK YOU for helping to share our books with families around the world!

GoodReads
Amazon
Indigo
Barnes and Noble
iBooks
Google Play
Kobo

laugh.learn.love
MotherButterfly.com